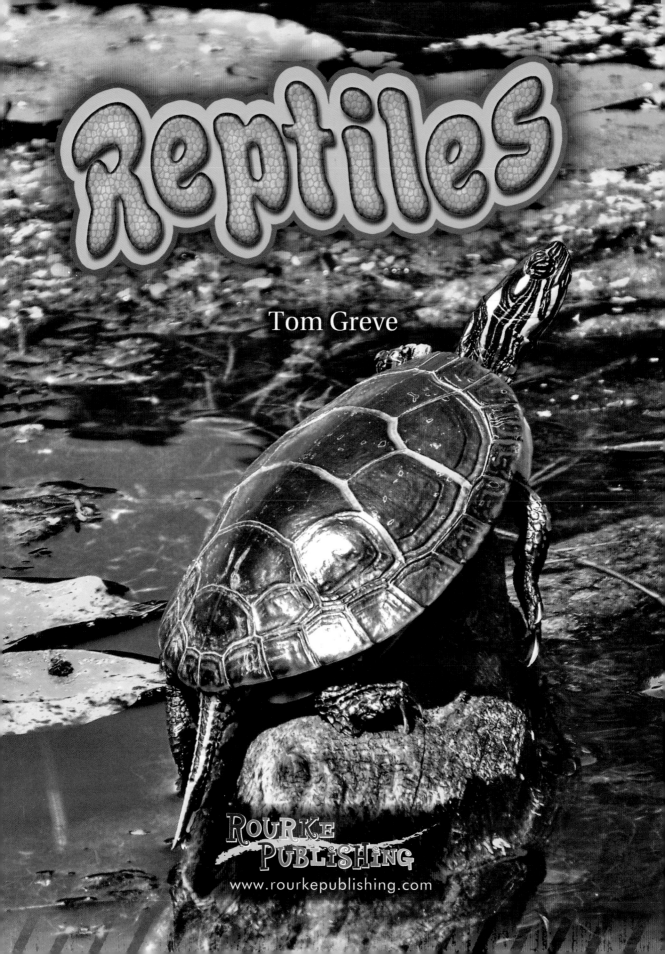

Reptiles

Tom Greve

ROURKE
PUBLISHING
www.rourkepublishing.com

www.rourkepublishing.com

PHOTO CREDITS: Cover: © luchschen; Title Page: © Philip Bobrow; Pages 2,3: © jmmf; Page 4: © Jullawadee; Pages 4,5: drbimages; Page 5: © Steve Allen; Page 6: © 916montgomery, Thanatham Piriyakarnjanakul, Thorsten Rust, Andy Heyward; Pages 6,7: © Lightscribe; Pages 8,9: © Peter Leahy, drbimages; Page 9: © Mgkuijpers; Page 10: © Island Effects, Susan Flashman; Pages 10,11: © drbimages; Page 11: © Nilanjan Bhattacharya, Craig Lopetz; Page 12: © Mgkuijpers; Page 13: © Eduard Kyslynskyy, Cathy Keifer; Pages 12,13: © drbimages; Page 14: © Bence Mate; Page 15: © Jakob Dam Knudsen, Martin Krause; Pages 16,17: © Surz01, drbimages; Page 18: © Angela Davis; Pages 18,19: © drbimages; Page 19: © Cameramannz; Page 20: © Alexshevchenko; Pages 20,21: © drbimages; Page 21: © Francis O\'Leary; Page 22: © Sam Lee; Pages 22,23: drbimages

Edited by Precious McKenzie

Cover Design by Renee Brady
Interior Design by Tara Raymo

Library of Congress Cataloging-in-Publication Data

Greve, Tom
 Reptiles / Tom Greve.
    p. cm. -- (Eye to Eye with Animals)
 ISBN 978-1-61741-775-7 (hard cover) (alk. paper)
 ISBN 978-1-61741-977-5 (soft cover)
 Library of Congress Control Number: 2011924820

Rourke Publishing
Printed in the United States of America, North Mankato, Minnesota
091610
091510LP-B

ROURKE PUBLISHING

www.rourkepublishing.com - rourke@rourkepublishing.com
Post Office Box 643328 Vero Beach, Florida 32964

Table of Contents

Chapter 1
Radical Reptiles

They are cold-blooded crawlers with tough skin and a backbone. **Reptiles** are among the most **adaptable** creatures on Earth. While most live on land, some prefer the water. They display a dizzying variety of self-defense capabilities, and some are among the most feared **predators** on Earth. But what reptiles have really mastered is the art of pacing themselves.

North American Alligator

CHILLING OUT!

▲ Reptiles are ectothermic which means they depend on the Sun for warmth and shade or water for cooling off. This also means they don't need to constantly eat in order to produce energy to stay warm.

Galapagos tortoises have ▶▶ two speeds: slow and stop. What they lack in quickness they make up for in longevity. They can live to be more than 100 years old. Because they were hunted as a food source for sailors in centuries past, they are now an endangered species.

RADICAL REPTILES

Found nowhere else on Earth besides the Galapagos Islands in the Pacific Ocean, the Galapagos tortoises look and behave differently based on which island they live on. This **diversity** shows how tortoises, reptiles, and animals in general can adapt to their specific **habitat**.

There are four major classes of living reptiles. Within these four groups there are many smaller divisions of **species.** While they may have slightly different habitats, diets, and survival skills, they are all reptiles.

Types of Reptiles

Turtles and Tortoises

Crocodilians

Snakes and Lizards

Tuataras

Reptiles generally live in warmer **environments**. They can live in or near oceans, rivers, swamps, jungles, and even deserts.

Reptile Range

Reptiles can be found on every continent on Earth except for Antarctica. It is too cold for reptiles to survive in Antarctica.

Chapter 2

Talking about Turtles

Turtles and tortoises have a bony shell. Some species live on land while others prefer the water. Some eat plants while others eat animals. All turtles and tortoises lay eggs and usually bury the eggs to protect them from predators until they hatch.

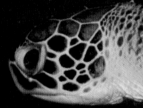

Unlike land-based tortoises and turtles, sea turtles have large front flippers for swimming. Even though they breathe air like we do, sea turtles can stay beneath the surface for long stretches of time.

The shells of turtles and tortoises are used as protection against predators. They pull their head as well as their legs or flippers inside the shell when they feel threatened.

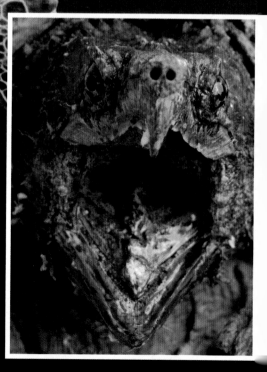

Instead of teeth, turtles and tortoises have hard-edged jaws that cut the plants or animals they eat.

Chapter 3
Cagey Crocs

Crocodilians are the largest and most dangerous types of reptiles. The crocodilian family includes crocodiles, alligators, caimans, and gharials. They're all **carnivores** with incredibly powerful jaws. They all lay eggs and spend long days sunning themselves in between their meals.

RADICAL REPTILES

Saltwater crocodiles are the only crocodilia reptile known to inhal the open ocean. They' been spotted hundred miles from shore.

KING CROC!

The saltwater crocodile is the largest of all crocodilians. They can grow to be 23 feet (7 meters) long and weigh more than a ton (1,000 kilograms).

Patient hunters, crocodilians attack with incredible ferocity. They can kill and eat **mammals** as large as horses or cattle. But once they succeed in getting a meal, they won't need another for weeks or even months.

◀◀ *Due to humans moving into their habitat, gharials, or fish-eating crocodiles, are now an endangered species. They are found in the wild only in parts of India and Nepal. They are identifiable by their long, narrow snouts.*

American Alligator

▲ *Like all reptiles, crocodilians have adapted to their habitat. The nostrils atop their snout allow them to breathe while they hide underwater looking for prey on the shore.*

Chapter 4
Slithering Snakes and Lizards

Mysterious and **exotic,** snakes and lizards make many people uncomfortable. Their appearance, habitat, and behaviors vary, but they all have scaly skin which they shed as they grow. They have also developed special features to use in their habitats for defense against predators, or to help them hunt for **prey.**

Timor python

▲ *Snakes never close their eyes. Instead of moveable eyelids, they have a special clear lens to keep their eyes moist and protected.*

Perhaps no single species of reptile has as many survival tricks up its scaly sleeve as the chameleon.

▲▲ *When hunting for insects to eat, chameleons make up for a lack of quickness by using an incredibly long, sticky tongue which they throw to catch prey in a heartbeat, like a retractable no-pest strip.*

To avoid predators, chameleons not only change colors to camouflage themselves, but their eyes rotate and focus separately from each other. This lets them see forward, backward, and side to side at any one time. ▶▶

Lizards and snakes are nature's magicians. Many are capable of amazing physical feats when they try to avoid predators or when they eat their prey.

RADICAL REPTILES

Seemingly defying the laws of physics, green basilisk lizards can run short distances on the surface of water without sinking.

Green basilisks have long toes on their rear feet with skin attachments that they use to slap against the water. This creates enough of an air pocket to prevent them from sinking as long as they move their feet fast enough.

All snakes are carnivores. Some snakes kill by biting and injecting toxic **venom** into their prey. Other snakes are constrictors. They attack by wrapping their long bodies around their prey and squeezing, or constricting, it to death. In either case, snakes swallow their prey whole. Many times, the prey is actually larger than the snake's head!

Python

◀◀ How do they do that? Thanks to stretchable head muscles and the ability to unhinge their jaws, snakes can open their mouths wide enough to swallow animals that appear too big for them to eat.

Anacondas are among ▶▶ the largest snakes on Earth and can grow to more than 30 feet (10 meters) in length. They are constrictors capable of swallowing large mammals , even humans, if they feel threatened.

Chapter 5

Misunderstood Monsters

Snakes and lizards have long been feared and, in some cases, worshipped by people. Their otherworldly appearance and bizarre physical abilities have awed and terrified humans throughout history. But snakes and lizards, like most animals, pose very little threat to humans.

> *It doesn't breathe fire, b[...] Komodo dragon is the w[...] largest lizard. They can g[...] 10 feet (3 meters) long a[...] up to 300 pounds (136 kil[...]*

RADICAL REPT[...]

Native to a few Indonesian Islands[...] Komodo dragon is a classic examp[...] reptilian efficiency. They'll patientl[...] for prey to cross their paths then s[...] into action, catching it and killing i[...] can eat 80 percent of their body we[...] in a single feeding, then not need a[...] meal for weeks.

Chapter 6
Tricky Tuataras

By far the smallest group is the tuataras. They look like lizards but they are not the same. They have skeletal differences and mate differently than lizards. They are **nocturnal** insect hunters who spend their days sunning themselves.

Tuataras are endangered due to non-native animals like dogs and rats eating their eggs. The dogs and rats arrived with humans from other parts of the world.

Although they once lived throughout New Zealand's main islands, tuataras now live only on a few small islands just to the north of New Zealand. Scientists say there are only about 50,000 tuataras left in the wild.

Chapter 7

Threats and Conservation

The greatest threat to reptile populations around the world is the destruction of their habitat by humans.

Human activities cause the most damage to reptiles, but humans are also involved in helping them survive. **Conservation** groups like the International Reptile Conservation Foundation work to ensure that threatened species of reptiles are protected along with their habitats.

Some reptiles are hunted by ▶▶ *humans for their skins. Other reptiles are captured and sold as pets.*

▼ *Conservation efforts are helping the Cayman Islands' blue iguana. This effort includes marking their habitat as protected land, thereby making logging, farming, or other human pursuits illegal.*

21

Reptiles are a varied and fascinating group of animals. They're exotic and cold-blooded, tough-skinned but vulnerable. Turtles, tortoises, crocodilians, snakes, lizards, and tuataras are all masters at adapting to the demands of their environments.

Humans moving into their habitats threaten some species. These curious, sometimes bizarre animals are natural treasures to be admired, not feared.

Glossary

adaptable (uh-DAPT-uh-buhl): able to change over time to accommodate a situation

carnivores (KAR-nuh-vorz): meat eaters

conservation (kon-sur-VAY-shuhn): the protection of valuable or rare things

diversity (duh-VURS-uh-tee): variety

environments (en-VYE-ruhn-muhntz): the places where an animal lives

exotic (eg-ZOT-ik): strange and fascinating

habitat (HAB-uh-tat): the place and natural conditions that an animal lives in

mammals (MAM-uhlz): any type of warm- blooded animal with a backbone

native (NAY-tiv): a certain place that an animal naturally lives

nocturnal (nok-TUR-nuhl): active at night

predators (PRED-uh-turz): animals that hunt other animals for food

prey (PRAY): an animal that is hunted by another animal for food

reptiles (REP-tilez): cold-blooded animals that crawl across the ground or creep on short legs

species (SPEE-seez): groups into which animals are classified

venom (VEN-uhm): poison produced by some snakes, injected into prey by biting

Index

Websites To Visit

Nationalgeographic.org

Sandiegozoo.org

NationalZoo.si.edu

WWF.org

IRCF.org

About the Author

Tom Greve lives in Chicago with his wife Meg and their children Madison and William. He loves the outdoors and loves to visit the reptile house at Lincoln Park Zoo.